They're POETS and They KNOW IT!

A Collection of 30 Timeless Poems

Scholastic Inc.

New York · Toronto · London · Auckland · Sydney
Mexico City · New Delhi · Hong Kong · Buenos Aires

Permissions

"Alone" from OH PRAY MY WINGS ARE GONNA FIT ME WELL by Maya Angelou. Copyright © 1975 by Maya Angelou. Reprinted by permission of Random House, Inc.

"As simple as that—," "So many breezes," and "Today and today" from SPRING OF MY LIFE by Kabayashi Issa, translated by Sam Hamill. Copyright © 1997 by Sam Hamill. Reprinted by arrangement with Shambhala Publications, Inc., Boston, MA www.shambhala.com

"Awful Ogre's Breakfast" from AWFUL OGRE'S AWFUL DAY by Jack Prelutsky. Copyright © 2001 by Jack Prelutsky. Used with the permission of Greenwillow Books, an imprint of HarperCollins Children's Books.

"I, Too, Sing America" from THE COLLECTED POEMS OF LANGSTON HUGHES edited by Arnold Rampersad with David Roessel, Associate Editor. Copyright 1994 by The Estate of Langston Hughes. Reprinted by permission of Alfred A. Knopf, a division of Random House, Inc.

"Teevee" from JAMBOREE: RHYMES FOR ALL TIMES by Eve Merriam. Copyright © 1962, 1964, 1966, 1973, 1984 by Eve Merriam. Used by permission of Marian Reiner.

"This Is Just to Say" from COLLECTED POEMS, 1909-1939, Volume I by William Carlos Williams. Copyright © 1938 by New Directions Publishing Corp. Reprinted by permission of New Directions Publishing Corp.

"The Dance of the Thirteen Skeletons" from NIGHTMARES, POEMS TO TROUBLE YOUR SLEEP by Jack Prelutsky. Copyright © 1976 by Jack Prelutsky. Used with the permission of Greenwillow Books, an imprint of HarperCollins Children's Books.

"Jabberwocky" is from *Through the Looking Glass, and What Alice Found There* by Lewis Caroll

"The Mouse's Tail" is from *Alice in Wonderland* by Lewis Carroll

ISBN-13: 978-0-545-03017-5
10 Book Pack ISBN: 0-545-03017-X
ISBN-10: B-0K5-03017-X

Interior Illustrations by Meredith Hamilton

12 11 10 9 8 7 6 5 4 3 2 1 7 8 9 10 11 12/0

Printed in the U.S.A.

First printing, October 2007

Table of Contents

Introduction

Poems tell stories and express feelings in creative ways...all through musical and rhythmical language. They can be short or long, funny or serious, sad or joyful. Some poems rhyme and others don't. Some have an obvious structure while others do not. But every poem is a work of art made entirely of words.

In this book you will find all sorts of poems by some of the world's greatest writers, including catchy limericks, elegant haiku, compelling narrative poems, playful free verse, and more.

From contemplating life in Robert Frost's poem "The Road Not Taken" to spouting all sorts of silly nonsense with Lewis Carroll, the poems in this book will challenge your mind, tickle your funny bone, and touch your heart.

Rhyming Poems

Rhyming sounds are everywhere—in song lyrics, tv advertisements, and poetry. Rhyme is a technique that creates rhythm using words that sound alike. Rhymed poems are a lot of fun to write. Pick any word, and think of all the words that rhyme with it. You'll be amazed at what you come up with!

A word is dead
When it is said,
Some say.
I say it just
Begins to live
That day.

—Emily Dickinson

The Road Not Taken

—Robert Frost

Two roads diverged in a yellow wood,
And sorry I could not travel both
And be one traveler, long I stood
And looked down one as far as I could
To where it bent in the undergrowth;

Then took the other, as just as fair,
And having perhaps the better claim,
Because it was grassy and wanted wear;
Though as for that, the passing there
Had worn them really about the same,

And both that morning equally lay
In leaves no step had trodden black.
Oh, I kept the first for another day!
Yet knowing how way leads on to way,
I doubted if I should ever come back.

I shall be telling this with a sigh
Somewhere ages and ages hence:
Two roads diverged in a wood, and I—
I took the one less traveled by,
And that has made all the difference.

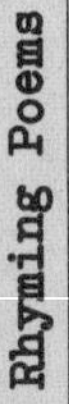

What Is Pink?

—*Christina Georgina Rossetti*

What is pink? a rose is pink
By a fountain's brink.
What is red? a poppy's red
In its barley bed.
What is blue? the sky is blue
Where the clouds float thro'.
What is white? a swan is white
Sailing in the light.
What is yellow? pears are yellow,
Rich and ripe and mellow.
What is green? the grass is green,
With small flowers between.
What is violet? clouds are violet
In the summer twilight.
What is orange? why, an orange,
Just an orange!

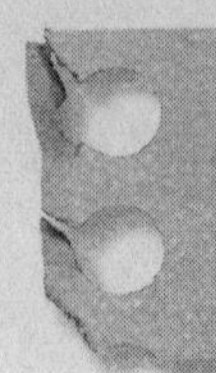

Alone

—*Maya Angelou*

Lying, thinking
Last night
How to find my soul a home
Where water is not thirsty
And bread loaf is not stone
I came up with one thing
And I don't believe I'm wrong
That nobody,
But nobody
Can make it out here alone.

Alone, all alone
Nobody, but nobody
Can make it out here alone.

There are some millionaires
With money they can't use
Their wives run round like banshees
Their children sing the blues
They've got expensive doctors
To cure their hearts of stone.
But nobody
No nobody
Can make it out here alone.

Alone, all alone
Nobody, but nobody
Can make it out here alone.

Now if you listen closely
I'll tell you what I know
Storm clouds are gathering
The wind is gonna blow
The race of man is suffering
And I can hear the moan,
Cause nobody
But nobody
Can make it out here alone.

Alone, all alone
Nobody, but nobody
Can make it out here alone.

Who Has Seen the Wind?

—Christina Georgina Rossetti

Who has seen the wind?
        Neither I nor you:
But when the leaves hang trembling,
        The wind is passing through.

Who has seen the wind?
        Neither you nor I:
But when the trees bow down their heads,
        The wind is passing by.

The Land of Nod

—Robert Louis Stevenson

From breakfast on through all the day
At home among my friends I stay,
But every night I go abroad
Afar into the land of Nod.

All by myself I have to go,
With none to tell me what to do—
All alone beside the streams
And up the mountain-sides of dreams.

The strangest things are there for me,
Both things to eat and things to see,
And many frightening sights abroad
Till morning in the land of Nod.

Try as I like to find the way,
I never can get back by day,
Nor can remember plain and clear
The curious music that I hear.

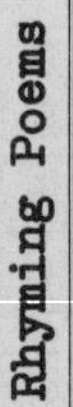

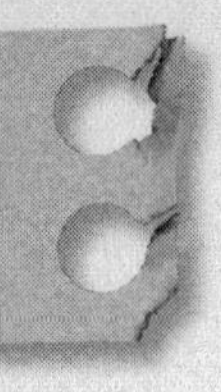

My Shadow

—Robert Louis Stevenson.

I have a little shadow that goes in and out with me,
And what can be the use of him is more than I can see.
He is very, very like me from the heels up to the head;
And I see him jump before me, when I jump into my bed.

The funniest thing about him is the way he likes to grow—
Not at all like proper children, which is always very slow;
For he sometimes shoots up taller like an india-rubber ball,
And he sometimes goes so little that there's none of him at all.

He hasn't got a notion of how children ought to play,
And can only make a fool of me in every sort of way.
He stays so close behind me, he's a coward you can see;
I'd think shame to stick to nursie as that shadow sticks to me!

One morning, very early, before the sun was up,
I rose and found the shining dew on every buttercup;
But my lazy little shadow, like an arrant sleepy-head,
Had stayed at home behind me and was fast asleep in bed.

Free Verse

If you are a rule breaker, free verse might be the poetry form for you. Free verse doesn't have to rhyme, but many free verse poems have their own patterns. Poets like to write in free verse because it gives them lots of freedom to express themselves.

The fog comes
on little cat feet.

It sits looking
over harbor and city
on silent haunches
and then moves on.

Chicago Poet

—Carl Sandburg

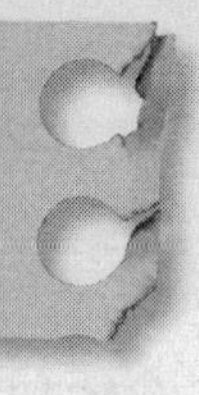

I SALUTED a nobody.
I saw him in a looking-glass.
He smiled—so did I.
He crumpled the skin on his forehead, frowning—so did I.
Everything I did he did.
I said, "Hello, I know you."
And I was a liar to say so.

Ah, this looking-glass man!
Liar, fool, dreamer, play-actor,
Soldier, dusty drinker of dust—
Ah! he will go with me
Down the dark stairway
When nobody else is looking,
When everybody else is gone.

He locks his elbow in mine,
I lose all—but not him.

Free Verse

The First Dandelion

—Walt Whitman

Simple and fresh and fair from winter's close emerging,
As if no artifice of fashion, business, politics, had ever been,
Forth from its sunny nook of shelter'd grass—innocent,
golden, calm as the dawn,
The spring's first dandelion shows its trustful face.

This Is Just to Say

—William Carlos Williams

I have eaten
the plums
that were in
the icebox

and which
you were probably
saving
for breakfast

Forgive me
they were delicious
so sweet
and so cold

I, Too, Sing America

—*Langston Hughes*

I, too, sing America.

I am the darker brother.
They send me to eat in the kitchen
When company comes,
But I laugh,
And eat well,
And grow strong.

Tomorrow,
I'll be at the table
When company comes.
Nobody'll dare
Say to me,
"Eat in the kitchen,"
Then.

Besides,
They'll see how beautiful I am
And be ashamed—

I, too, am America.

Free Verse

Limericks

Limericks are usually funny or silly, and always have five lines. When you write a limerick of your own, think of each poem as a very short story.

There was a young lady whose chin
resembled the point of a pin;
so she had it made sharp,
and purchased a harp,
and played several tunes with her chin.

There was an old man who supposed
that the street door was partially closed;
but some very large rats
ate his coats and his hats,
while that futile old gentleman dozed.

There was an old man with a beard,
who said, "It is just as I feared!
Two owls and a hen,
four larks and a wren,
have all built their nests in my beard!"

There is a young lady whose nose,
continually prospers and grows.
When it grew out of sight,
she exclaimed in a fright,
"Oh! Farewell to the end of my nose!"

There was a young lady whose eyes
were unique as to color and size.
When she opened them wide,
people all turned aside,
and started away in surprise.

There was an old man in a tree
whose whiskers were lovely to see;
but the birds of the air
pluck'd them perfectly bare
to make themselves nests in that tree.

—Edward Lear

Narrative Poems

A narrative poem tells a story, and is longer than most forms of poetry. It can rhyme, but it doesn't have to. Narrative poems can also have patterns that create rhythm. Each line might have the same number of syllables or the stanzas might have the same number of lines.

The Dance of the Thirteen Skeletons

—Jack Prelutsky

In a snow-enshrouded graveyard
gripped by winter's bitter chill,
not a single soul is stirring,
all is silent, all is still
till a distant bell tolls midnight
and the spirits work their will.

For emerging from their coffins
buried deep beneath the snow,
thirteen bony apparitions
now commence their spectral show,
and they gather in the moonlight
undulating as they go.

> And they'll dance in their bones,
> in their bare bare bones,
> with the click and the clack
> and the chitter and the chack
> and the clatter and the chatter
> of their bare bare bones.

They shake their flimsy shoulders
and they flex their fleshless knees
and they nod their skulls in greeting
in the penetrating breeze
as they form an eerie circle
near the gnarled and twisted trees.

They link their spindly fingers
as they promenade around
casting otherworldly shadows
on the silver-mantled ground
and their footfalls in the snowdrift

And they dance in their bones,
in their bare bare bones,
with the click and the clack
and the chitter and the chack
and the clatter and the chatter
of their bare bare bones.

The thirteen grinning skeletons
continue on their way
as to strains of soundless music
they begin to swing and sway
and they circle ever faster
in their ghastly roundelay.

Faster, faster ever faster
and yet faster now they race,
winding, whirling, ever swirling
in the frenzy of their pace
and they shimmer in the moonlight
as they spin themselves through space.

And they dance in their bones,
in their bare bare bones,
with the click and the clack
and the chitter and the chack
and the clatter and the chatter
of their bare bare bones.

Then as quickly as it started
their nocturnal dance is done
for the bell that is their signal
loudly tolls the hour of one
and they bow to one another
in their bony unison.

Then they vanish to their coffins
by their ghostly thoroughfare
and the emptiness of silence
once more fills the frosted air
and the snows that mask their footprints
show no sign that they were there.

But they danced in their bones,
in their bare bare bones,
with the click and the clack
and the chitter and the chack
and the clatter and the chatter
of their bare bare bones.

Annabel Lee

—Edgar Allan Poe

It was many and many a year ago,
In a kingdom by the sea,
That a maiden there lived whom you may know
By the name of Annabel Lee;
And this maiden she lived with no other thought
Than to love and be loved by me.

I was a child and she was a child,
In this kingdom by the sea:
But we loved with a love that was more than love—
I and my Annabel Lee;
With a love that the winged seraphs of heaven
Coveted her and me.

And this was the reason that, long ago,
In this kingdom by the sea,
A wind blew out of a cloud, chilling
My beautiful Annabel Lee;
So that her high-born kinsmen came
And bore her away from me,
To shut her up in a sepulchre
In this kingdom by the sea.

The angels, not half so happy in heaven,
Went envying her and me—
Yes!—that was the reason (as all men know,
In this kingdom by the sea)
That the wind came out of the cloud by night,
Chilling and killing my Annabel Lee.

But our love it was stronger by far than the love
Of those who were older than we—
Of many far wiser than we—
And neither the angels in heaven above,
Nor the demons down under the sea,
Can ever dissever my soul from the soul
Of the beautiful Annabel Lee,

For the moon never beams without bringing me dreams
Of the beautiful Annabel Lee;
And the stars never rise but I feel the bright eyes
Of the beautiful Annabel Lee;
And so, all the night-tide, I lie down by the side
Of my darling—my darling—my life and my bride,
In the sepulchre there by the sea,
In her tomb by the sounding sea.

The Owl and the Pussy-cat

—*Edward Lear*

I

The Owl and the Pussy-cat went to sea
    In a beautiful pea green boat,
They took some honey, and plenty of money,
    Wrapped up in a five pound note.
The Owl looked up to the stars above,
    And sang to a small guitar,
"O lovely Pussy! O Pussy my love,
    What a beautiful Pussy you are,
        You are,
        You are!
What a beautiful Pussy you are!"

II

Pussy said to the Owl, "You elegant fowl!
    How charmingly sweet you sing!
O let us be married! too long we have tarried:
    But what shall we do for a ring?"
They sailed away, for a year and a day,
    To the land where the Bong-tree grows
And there in a wood a Piggy-wig stood
    With a ring at the end of his nose,
        His nose,
        His nose,
With a ring at the end of his nose.

III

"Dear pig, are you willing to sell for one shilling
Your ring?" Said the Piggy, "I will."
So they took it away, and were married next day
By the Turkey who lives on the hill.
They dined on mince, and slices of quince,
Which they ate with a runcible spoon;
And hand in hand, on the edge of the sand,
They danced by the light of the moon,
The moon,
The moon,
They danced by the light of the moon.

The Mouse's Tail

—Lewis Carroll

Fury said to a mouse,
That he met in the
house, "Let us
both go to law:
I will prosecute
you—Come, I'll
take no denial;
We must have
a trial: For
really this
morning I've
nothing to do."
Said the mouse
to the cur,
"Such a trial,
dear Sir, With
no jury or
judge, would
be wasting
our breath."
"I'll be
judge, I'll
be jury,"
Said cunning
old Fury:
"I'll try
the whole
cause, and
condemn
you
to
death."

Concrete Poems

Concrete poems are a lot of fun to read, but even more fun to write. These shape poems are spaced to form pictures of what the poem is about! Can you spot the shape of this poem?

Teevee

—Eve Merriam

In the house
of Mr. and Mrs. Spouse
he and she
would watch teevee
and never a word
between them spoken
until the day
the set was broken.

Then "How do you do?"
said he to she,
"I don't believe
that we've met yet.
Spouse is my name
What's yours?" he asked.

"Why mine's the same!"
said she to he,
"Do you suppose that we could be—?"

But the set came suddenly right about,
and so they never did find out.

Humorous Poems

A poem doesn't have to be serious. Sometimes the poet uses goofy rhymes, silly-sounding words, and odd subjects to make the reader howl with laughter.

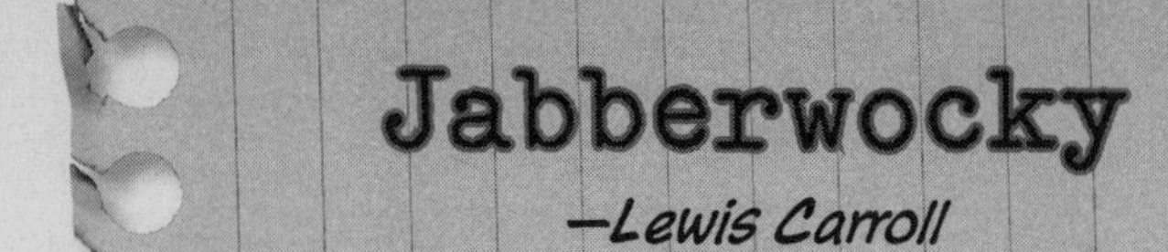

Jabberwocky

—Lewis Carroll

'Twas brillig, and the slithy toves
        Did gyre and gimble in the wabe;
All mimsy were the borogoves,
        And the mome raths outgrabe.

"Beware the Jabberwock, my son!
        The jaws that bite, the claws that catch!
Beware the Jubjub bird, and shun
        The frumious Bandersnatch!'"

He took his vorpal sword in hand:
        Long time the manxome foe he sought--
So rested he by the Tumtum tree,
        And stood awhile in thought.

And as in uffish thought he stood,
        The Jabberwock, with eyes of flame,
Came whiffling through the tulgey wood,
        And burbled as it came!

One, two! One, two! And through and through
        The vorpal blade went snicker-snack!
He left it dead, and with its head
        He went galumphing back.

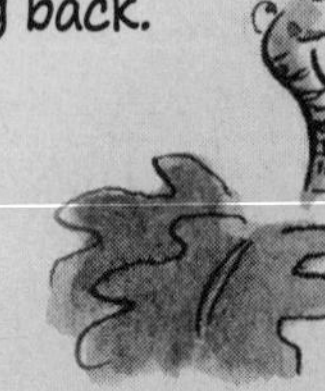

"And hast thou slain the Jabberwock?
Come to my arms, my beamish boy!
O frabjous day! Callooh! Callay!"
He chortled in his joy.

'Twas brillig, and the slithy toves
Did gyre and gimble in the wabe;
All mimsy were the borogoves,
And the mome raths outgrabe.

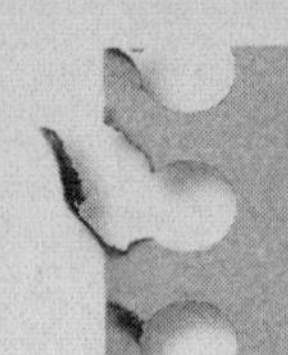

The Rose Family

—Robert Frost

The rose is a rose,
And was always a rose.
But the theory now goes
That the apple's a rose,
And the pear is, and so's
The plum, I suppose.
The dear only knows
What will next prove a rose.
You, of course, are a rose—
But were always a rose.

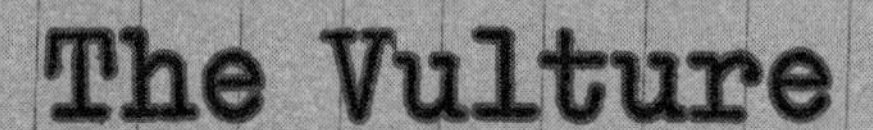

The Vulture

—Hilaire Belloc

The Vulture eats between his meals,
And that's the reason why
He very, very rarely feels
As well as you and I.

His eye is dull, his head is bald,
His neck is growing thinner.
Oh! What a lesson for us all
To only eat at dinner!

Awful Ogre's Breakfast

—*Jack Prelutsky*

Oh breakfast, lovely breakfast,
You're the meal I savor most.
I sip a bit of gargoyle bile
And chew some ghoul on toast.

I linger over scrambled legs,
Complete with pickled feet,
Then finish with a piping bowl
Of steamy *SCREAM OF WHEAT.*

Haiku

A haiku is a short poem invented in Japan. It often describes nature with very simple observations about the elegant world around us. A haiku usually consists of three unrhymed lines of 5, 7, and 5 syllables.

As simple as that—
spring has finally arrived
with a pale blue sky

So many breezes
wander through my summer room:
but never enough

Today and today
also—a kite entangled
in a gnarled tree

—*Issa*

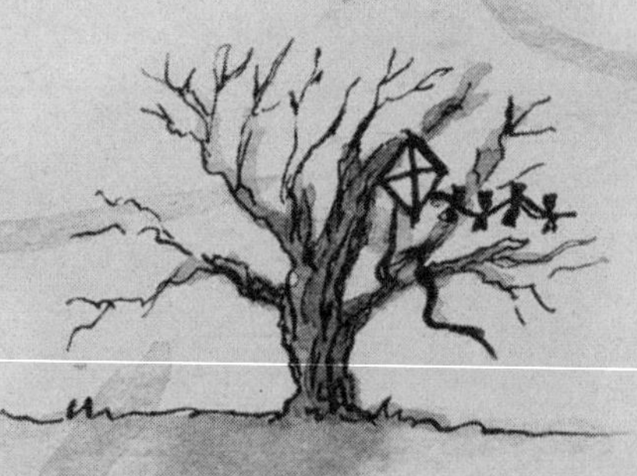